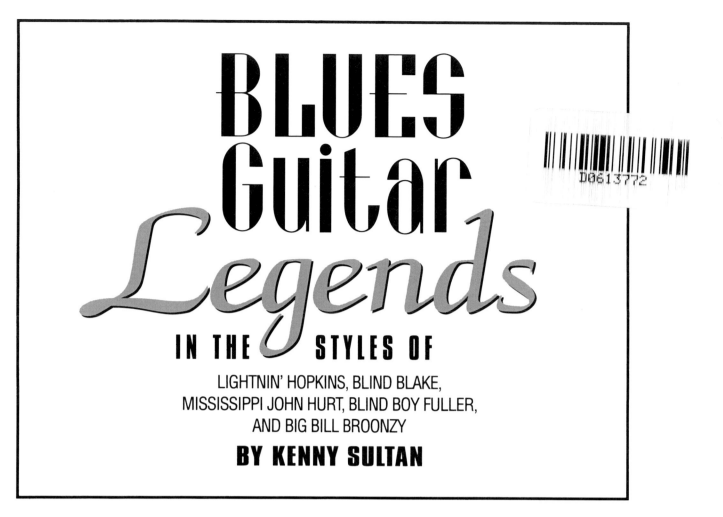

BLUES Guitar Legends

IN THE STYLES OF

LIGHTNIN' HOPKINS, BLIND BLAKE,
MISSISSIPPI JOHN HURT, BLIND BOY FULLER,
AND BIG BILL BROONZY

BY KENNY SULTAN

Thank Yous
I would like to thank Rick Powell of Virtuoso Guitars, Richard at Santa Cruz Guitar Company, the gang at National Reso-phonic Guitars and Triplett Harps. Special Thanks to Irv and Jean, Tom Ball, Scoop, and the ladies at Folk Mote Music.

SAN 683 8022
ISBN 1-57424-01503

To access audio visit:
www.halleonard.com/mylibrary

Enter Code
1376-5794-1691-6642

Cover Photo: Jeff Brouws
Recording: Songwriter 'N' Musicians recording studio, Santa Barbara, CA
Engineer: Cory Orosco
Guitar Grids - Kenneth Warfield
Music Notation - Dave Celentano
Paste-up - Cindy Middlebrook
Layout & Production - Ron Middlebrook

Contents

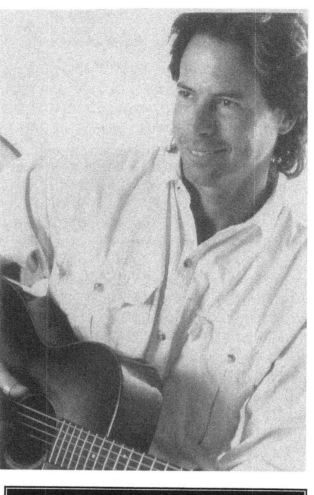

Kenny Sultan

Kenny Sultan has been playing guitar since the age of seven. Soon thereafter, his brother introduced him to the Blues of T-Bone Walker and Lightnin' Hopkins. The effect was permanent.

A noted teacher, he has taught music, guitar and blues at the College level. Kenny has also conducted workshops and seminars throughout the country.

He has six albums to his credit with his partner Tom Ball and has appeared as a sideman on numerous recordings by other artists.

He currently resides in Santa Barbara, California.

Foreword

Well, here we go again. It's time for our third volume in a series of blues books for Centerstream Publications. If you have any of the earlier editions welcome back, if you are new I'm glad you are here.

The concept for this book is unique. I'll be attempting to teach you my loose interpretations of five legendary bluesmens music. In the end I hope this enables you to develop an original style of your own. In my many years of teaching I've discovered an abundance of publications that have exact note for note transcriptions of original blues songs. Attempting to play these was a nightmare. I found that in order to do things exactly, there was no feeling or emotion left in the music. Come on, can anyone really play like Lightnin' Hopkins? The best you can do is take the emotion from the original and do your own thing. How many of you have spent hours trying to learn that one mystery note and have never gotten it to sound right? I say relax, get as close as you can, and go from there.

I've taken some liberties with the music in this book. These songs are not even close to being note for note renditions of the originals. I know some blues purists are going to freak out but again, this is primarily a book to help you develop your own style. If I haven't bothered to be precise, I don't expect you to either. Feel free to add and subtract licks when you want. This isn't classical music or brain surgery. Live a little!

Finally, I must give credit where credit is due, and that's to the original blues artists. I would never think of taking anything away from them. Without seeing, listening, and learning from them, I would probably still be playing *"Last Train to Clarksville"* by the Monkees. This is why you should listen to as much original music of these artists as possible. It's the only way to see what's really happening. Remember they are the legends!

All right, are you ready?
Remember to work with the accompanying audio, it's very important. Also don't forget my four blues rules:

1. Have fun.
2. Play loose.
3. Play with feeling.
4. Don't worry about mistakes.

See ya,
Kenny Sultan

Sam "Lightnin" Hopkins

Our first stylist is Sam "Lightnin" Hopkins. He is my favorite blues player. I love the soul that comes through in his playing. He was born in Centerville, Texas on March 15, 1912. His guitar style was influenced by many of the Texas bluesman, most notably Blind Lemon Jefferson and his cousin Texas Alexander. Lightnin's association with Jefferson and Alexander helped mold his own distinctive blues style. His guitar form is very free, almost disorganized. That's why I like him so much.

Sam "Lightnin" Hopkins

I've tried to smooth out his style somewhat in my playing. What might sound incredible for Lightnin', would sound like mistakes for me. While it's cool for him to play 10 1/2 bar blues, it would sound like I didn't know what I was doing. Now I'm not saying I don't go out on a limb now and then, but for jamming purposes it's best to stick to the 12 bar format. This is what I've done for his section.

Here are some tricks I use to sound more like the man.

1. If you're striking more than one string at a time in either the bass or treble, try brushing or strumming the strings instead of picking them individually. (check the CD).

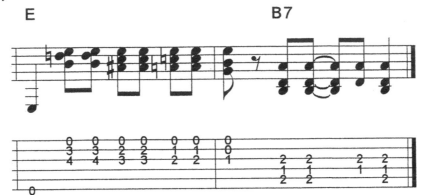

Play loose during these sections. You don't need to hit all the strings.

2. Play everything with a shuffle feel.
No straight eighth notes. *Swing it!* shuffle feel

3. The pinkie can be released from the first position B7 chord on occasion. This enables the B string to sound clear for Lightnin's standard B7 lick.

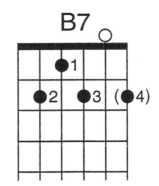

or

4. The bending and sliding of strings.
This will add a lot of feeling to your sound

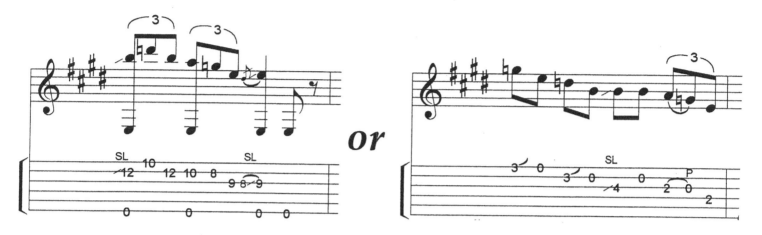

or

5. Listen to as much Lightnin' Hopkins material as possible.
This is the only way to try to capture his sound.

These are the notes (in no particular order) that Lightnin' used regularly. Feel free to improvise, let the blues be your guide.

Have you had enough advice? Let's get on to the music.
Be sure to listen to the accompaniment tracks to get the proper feel.

Our first song gives us a good (rhythmic) foundation in which to build upon. It's basically your normal E shuffle with some Lightnin' flavor added. The only measures where you need to make the full chords are in 9, 11, and 12. Remember the pinkie is optional for the B7 chord. Good luck!

Lightnin' Hopkins style

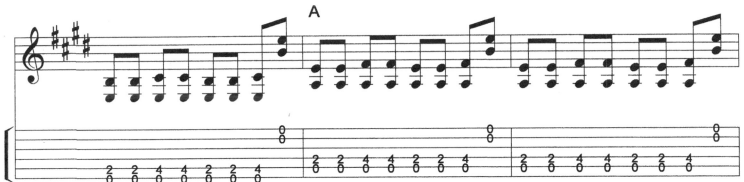

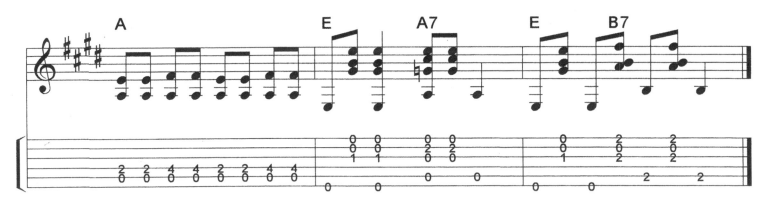

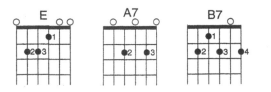

This is one of my favorite numbers.
Play this with a relaxed feel. Make the full chords except for measures 10 and 11.

Lightnin' Hopkins style
medium tempo 1

This song is pretty loose.
The only time you need to make any chords would be for measures 9, 11, and 12.
Otherwise it's all lead style, so go for it! <u>Remember the shuffle feel.</u>

Lightnin' Hopkins style
medium tempo 2

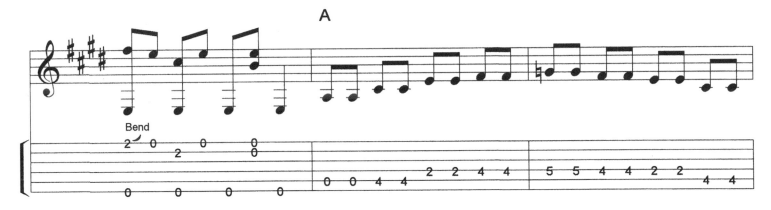

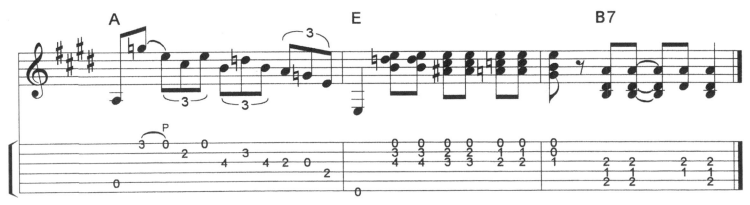

Get ready to move up the neck!

This tune uses the upper register box for the E chord. The bends in measures 3 and 4 are difficult so be sure to listen to the audio. Don't worry about playing exactly what's written This song is more feeling than technique. Play loose!.

Lightnin' Hopkins style
medium tempo 3

Our first slow song!

It's time to relax and proceed at a more leisurely pace. Check it out and we'll talk about it when you're through.

Lightnin' Hopkins style   slow 1

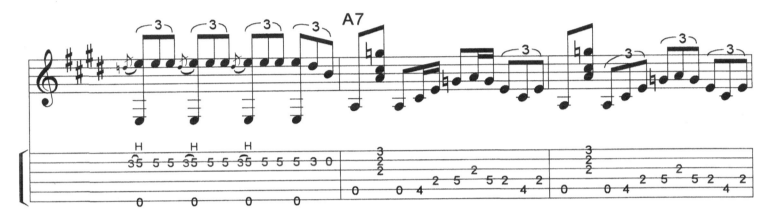

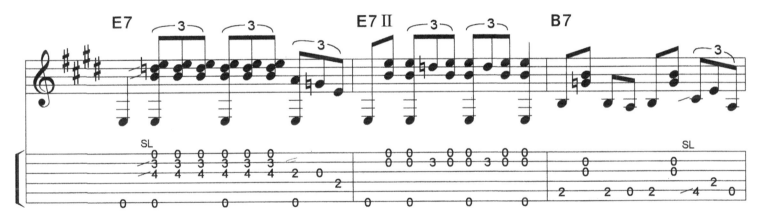

How did it go?

Bars 4, 5, and 6 are tricky. The hammer-on in bar 4 is very quick. I call it a grace hammer. Listen to the audio to get a feel for it. Measures 5 and 6 release the A7 chord after one beat. This enables you to play the bass run after it without permanently damaging your left hand.

12

This slow blues uses the same upper registar E box we used earlier in the book. You don't need to play it exactly as written. Have a beer and relax. Try to make the full chords in measures 5, 11 and 12. Have fun with this one.

Lightnin' Hopkins style
slow 2

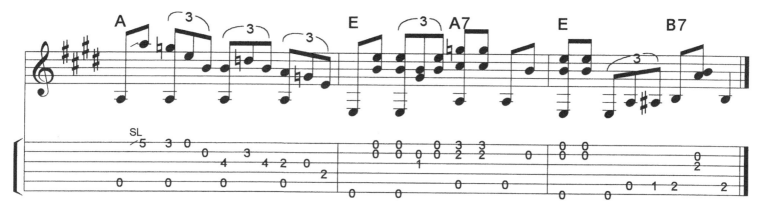

This song should pose no problem except for the bend in measure 4.
Listen to the recording for help.

Lightnin' Hopkins style
slow 3

Our final Lightnin' Hopkins style song is in the key of A. Although E was his favorite key, he also played some cool things in A. Here's what I remember.

Lightnin' Hopkins style *slow 4*

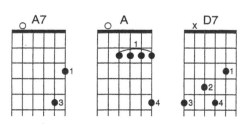

Blind Blake

Very little is known about Blind Blake but he was one of the most popular artists to record in the twenty's. He came from Tampa, Florida and was one of the most prominent east coast stylists to emerge from that area. His guitar style is incredibly complicated. It is

highly syncopated with a complex right hand technique. He would roll and often double-time his bass which gave his guitar playing a sound somewhat reminiscent to that of a piano. I've included most of the rolls but I've left out a lot of the double-time bass notes. I've never found anyone who could really play them right, including myself.

The songs in this section are in the key of G and C. These were Blakes favorite keys. He rarely played in A and rarer yet in E, which is unique for a bluesman.

For this section I've taken the liberty to change some things around to fit my style (i.e. double-time bass).

Hopefully I have retained the spirit of the Blakes music. Check it out.

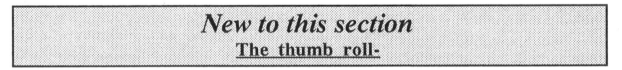

New to this section
The thumb roll-

Get ready because this technique is a regular feature of Blakes' songs. This is my interpretation of it. Be sure to check the fingering and listen to the recording to get the proper syncopation.

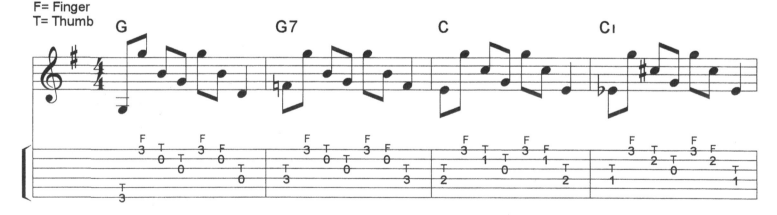

Our first Blake song puts us in the key of G.
Things to look out for
1. The bass walk between the D chord and G chord throughout the song.
2. The thumb rolls - the chord changes are difficult so take your time.
3. The walkdown between the G chord and E7 chord near the end of song.
   Use your thumb if you want on the bass string.
Remember, using an alternating bass means a lighter feel to the music.

That'll Never Happen No More

Blind Blake
arranged by Kenny Sultan

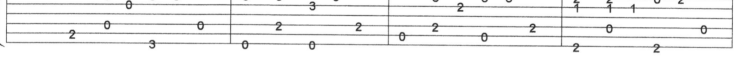

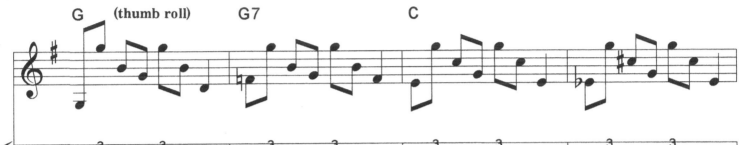

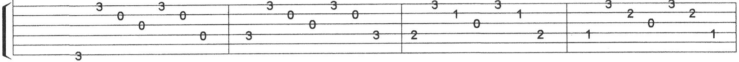

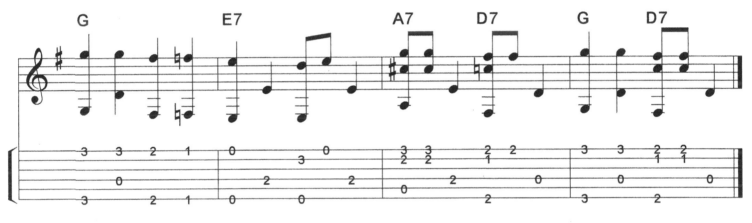

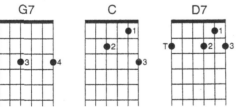

August 25, 1928

18

Blakes Breakdown is the consummate Blind Blake song.
It includes many of his trademark licks. I suggest you take it one section at a time.
Things to look out for
1. Obviously the thumb rolls. You'll find many.
2. The strum on the Ab7 and F chords. Check the recording.
3. The bass walk/treble finger roll for the C chord in bar 11, section I. I use the
    corresponding finger on my left hand to match the fret number. i.e. third
    finger for the 3rd fret, second finger for the 2nd fret etc.
4. New chord formations. Check the charts.

Blakes Breakdown

shuffle feel

Blind Blake
arranged by Kenny Sultan

section 1

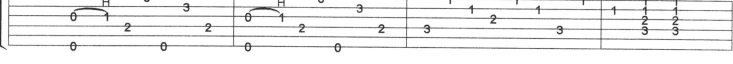

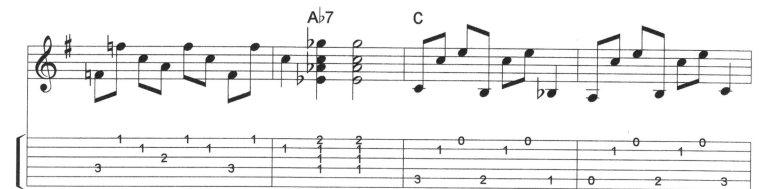

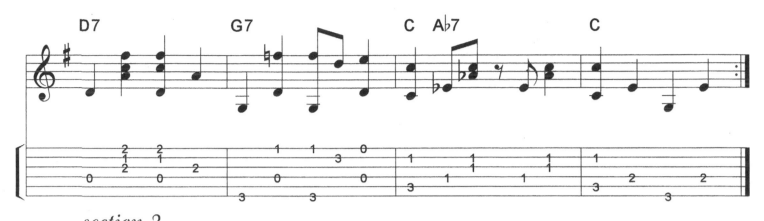

section 2

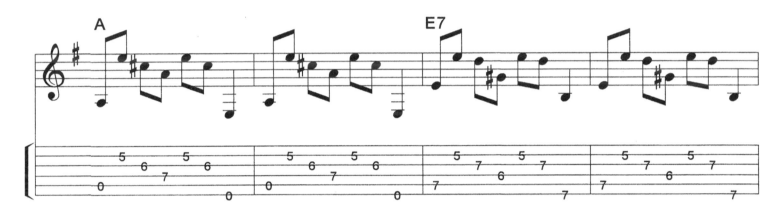

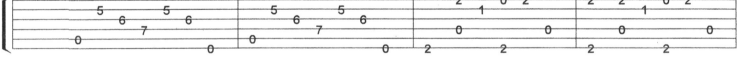

section 3

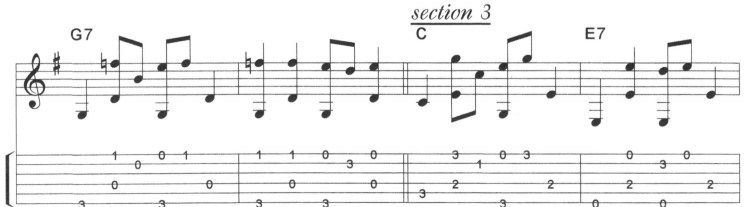

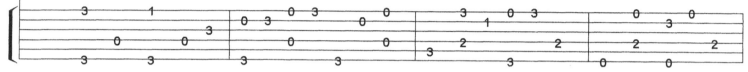

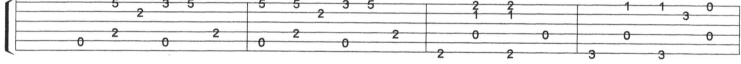

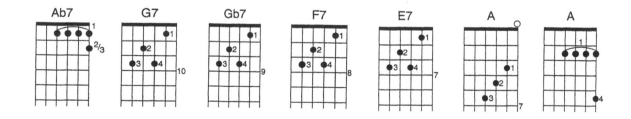

This song is from my album entitled "Filthy Rich". It has a definite Blake feel to it.
There is a tricky slide on the G chord. Check out the **recording**.

Six Reasons

music by
Kenny Sultan

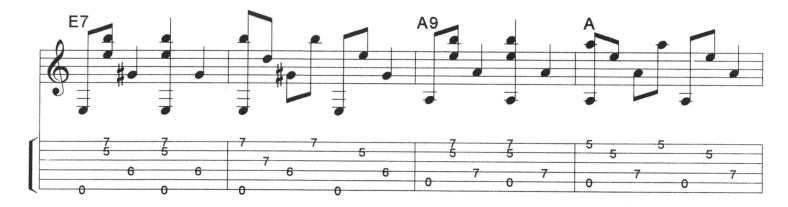

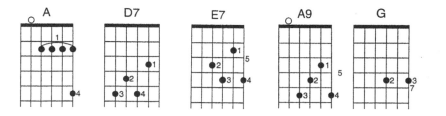

Mississippi John Hurt

John Hurt was born in Mississippi in 1895. His style differs drastically from other Mississippi bluesman. His melodic clarity is unique to that region. He relies on an alternating bass which supplies the rhythm while the treble strings pick out the melody. He played with a very light touch and didn't use fingerpicks. One of his trademarks was to play the melody line against two open bass strings. Sometimes this does not make perfect sense musically but it creates an interesting effect.

Mississippi John Hurt, 1963

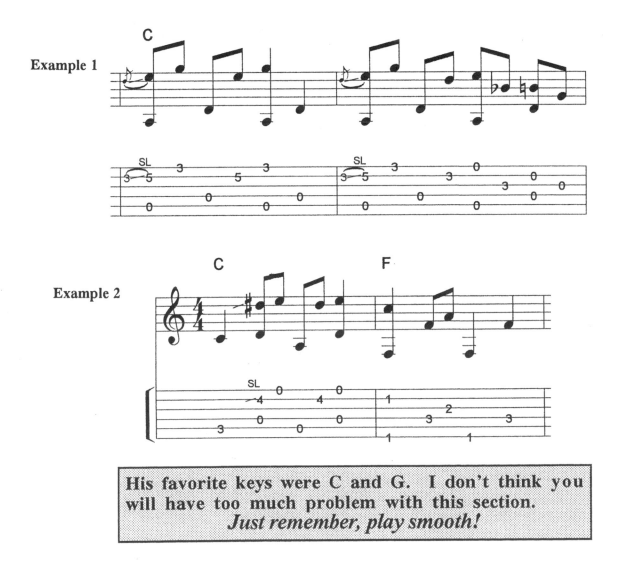

His favorite keys were C and G. I don't think you will have too much problem with this section. *Just remember, play smooth!*

24

Our first John Hurt tune is three similar sections played with different variations,
(Creole Belle - Richland Woman licks)
I'll explain each section separately.
This first one is fairly easy, just watch out for the thumb wrap F chord.

John Hurt style 1

This section is more difficult than the first.
There are more melody notes and a tough hammer-on in measure 2. Good luck!

John Hurt style 2

shuffle feel

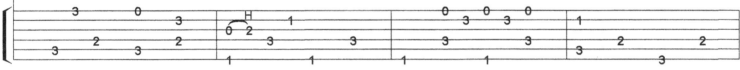

Our final variation on our first tune has a strange but beautiful melody played over the C and F chords. Check out the open bass strings.

John Hurt 3

Can't Be Satisfied is basically a G blues played "John Hurt" style.
Again check out the open strings in the bass on the C and D chords.
Listen to the accompanying audio track to get a feel for the slides.

Can't Be Satisfied 1
John Hurt style

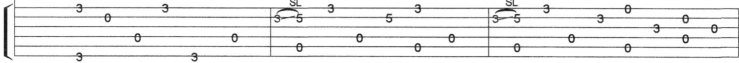

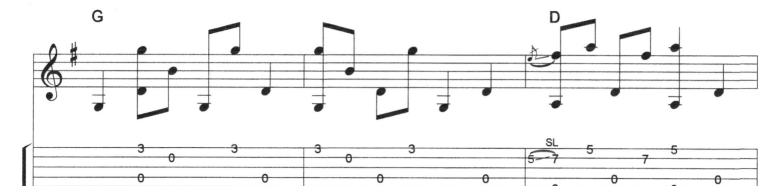

Can't Be Satisfied 2
John Hurt style

shuffle feel

Fulton Allen was to become the best-known and probably most influential of all bluesmen from the Southeast. As Blind Boy Fuller (he became blind about eight years before he began to record) he cut 130 titles, all of which were released in the six years before his premature death in 1941, at the age of thirty-three.

below: Blind Boy Fuller's manager J.B. Long poses in front of his Kingston, North Carolina, record store for a 1934 newspaper photo. The photo was captioned: "5,606 records at one time. Largest shipment ever received in a North Carolina store.

One of the two known photographs of Blind Boy Fuller

Our first Blind Boy Fuller song uses the classic VI, II, V, I ragtime chord progression. Sounds impressive doesn't it? The tune itself should pose no problem except for maybe the "A" chord. It's quite a stretch. I've included a substitute turnaround at the end of the song. If you prefer you can use this in place of the last four measures.

Wabash Rag Blind Boy Fuller style

Chords for Wabash Rag 2

Wabash Rag 2

I've always enjoyed playing this song.
There are plenty of new chords so be sure to review the charts.

Keep On Truckin' Mama
Blind Boy Fuller style

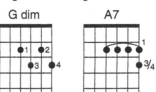

Keep On Truckin' Mama 2

Big Bill Broonzy

Big Bill Broonzy was born in Mississippi in 1898. He originally played fiddle but put this down to play guitar. Bill's guitar style was more urban sounding than most anyone else from the delta at that time. In most of his blues his guitar would be used solely as a response to his voice. Since my voice stinks, I've stuck to his rag/blues for this section. I must admit I've taken incredible liberties with his style and since that's the premise of this book I feel it's okay. Bill rarely used an alternating bass, I use it exclusively. I could never get the monotone bass to swing enough. There are other things I've changed as well which you'll see when we get to the music.

KINGSWAY HALL, LONDON

LONDON JAZZ CLUB
PROUDLY PRESENT A
RECITAL
BLUES • FOLK SONGS • BALLADS
by the Famous American Singer

"BIG" BILL BROONZY
Saturday, September 22nd, 1951

COLUMBIA
Mfrd. under U.S. Pat. No. 1,702,554 and Pat. Pending. Trade-Marks Reg. U.S. Pat. Off.–Marcas Registradas. Made in U.S.A.
For perfect tone use Columbia Needles
37088
(C 4308)
TELL ME BABY
Blues Singer with Instrumental Acc.
- Broonzy -
BIG BILL and his
CHICAGO FIVE

BIG BILL
NATIONAL

Long Tall Mama might not sound at all like the original since its been years since I've heard it. Consider this just a cool C rag/blues. The C chord in the first four measures should be played loose since the fingers never stay in one place for long. The F chord in measures 5 and 6 can be a problem. You can make this with a thumb wrap or a barre. I prefer the thumb wrap. There is a tricky bass walk between bars 6 and 7. If it's too difficult, use your normal F and C bass. Finally look out for the G bass run at the end (listen to the recording).

Long Tall Mama

The next three tunes are just a improvisation on Long Tall Mama. Remember they are just my interpretation of C blues played with Big Bill influences. One helpful strategy for this section is bailing out or releasing the chord forms when necessary. I recommend using your thumb and finger for the first four bars.

Big Bill style 1

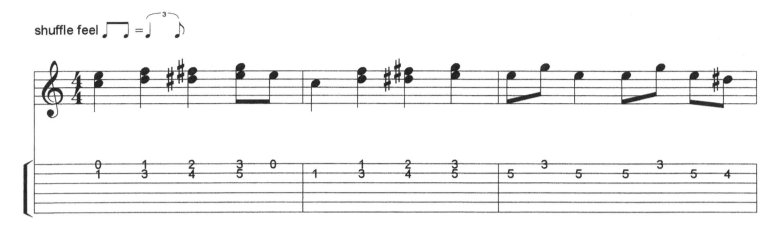

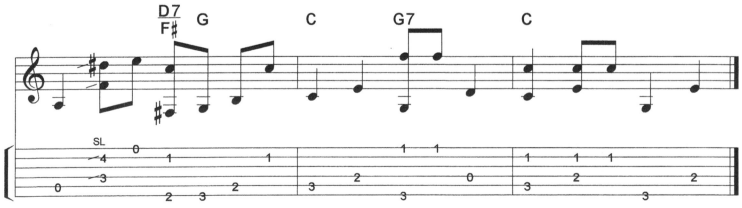

This section contains some cool lead lines and a funky diminished chord run. Don't forget to use your right hand thumb if you need to speed up the runs. I find a combination of thumb and fingers work best.

Big Bill style 2

Our final C improv is pretty much the same old, same old. I would release the C chord in the
first few bars and check out the chord charts for the new chords.

Big Bill 3

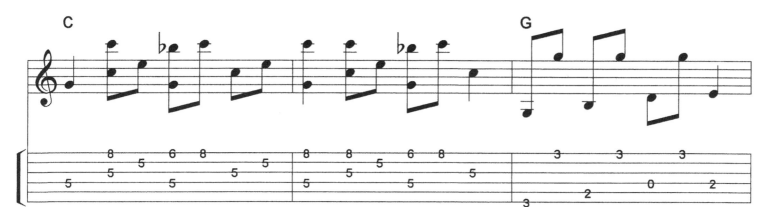

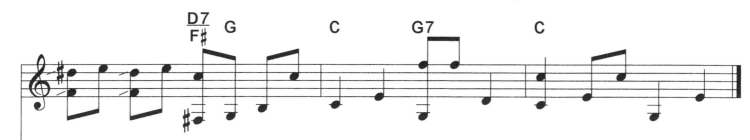

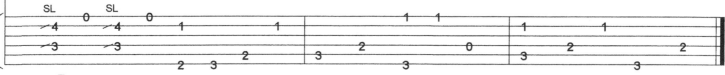

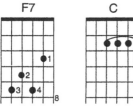

39

This is an original song that's on my CD entitled *"Too Much Fun"*. This is the only non-ragtime blues in this section. I've included it here because of the lick I stole from Big Bill that occurs in measures 3, 4 and 7, 8. Bill played the lick originally in G, and I just transposed it to A. It's very difficult. This song definitely has its quirks. The diminished chords, the double time bass, the various runs etc., all make this arrangement quite unusual. Listening to the CD is a must. May the music Gods' be with you.

Your Mind Is In The Gutter

by Tom Ball and
Kenny Sultan

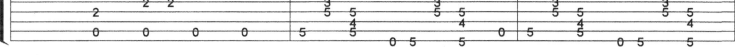

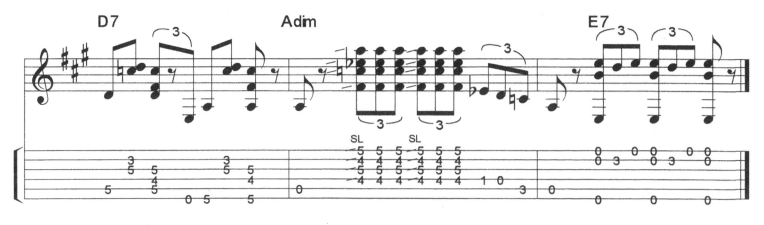

Your Mind Is In The Gutter 2

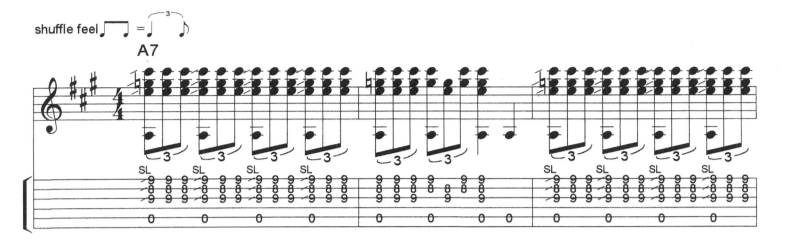

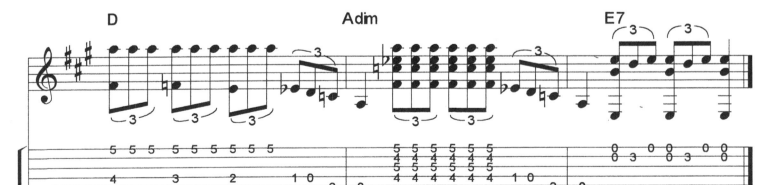

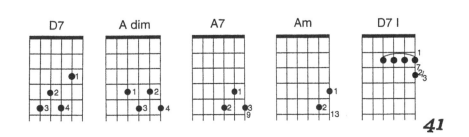

This song has always been a favorite of mine. The music is basically a combination of Big Bills version, Jim Kweskins's version and my own translation. Add what you want to it and we'll have a big stew!

Bill Bailey

Bill Bailey (continued)

Conclusion

Well, that's it! I hope you are on your way to developing your own funky style of guitar playing. If this book proved too difficult, check out my other books or videos from Centerstream Publications. If you want to add to your CD collection, I have five albums out with my partner Tom Ball, an excellent harmonica player/vocalist. We cover a wide variety of blues styles on these recordings. They are available from your better record stores, Flying Fish Records, or from myself:

Kenny Sultan - P.O. Box 20156 - Santa Barbara, CA 93120

Feel free to write me if you have any questions about this book.

Tom Ball & Kenny Sultan, Belgium Rock and Blues Festival

Tom Ball, George Thorogood, & Kenny Sultan

Finally I've left you with a small taste of my next book. It will be another style book concentrating on Rev. Gary Davis and other bluesmen. Enjoy "Buck Dance" and good luck with your playing.

Buck Dance 1

Buck Dance 2

Buck Dance 3

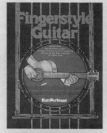